Relationship Revelations

From Hunt & Bunny's Adventures in Wonderland

Hunt Henion

Shift Awareness Books
For a Better Perspective
www.shiftawareness.com

Contents

Introduction to Love
by Harold W. Becker

When we bring unconditional love into our personal, professional, community and family lives, we begin the journey of restoring wholeness and happiness to our planetary adventure. *Relationship Revelations* is a genuine story of unconditional love filled with strength, courage, intimacy and honesty. Hunt's candid chronicle of his unfolding experience with Bunny is an inspiring portrayal of our beautifully diverse human nature. Each page opens our hearts and minds to a deeper understanding of the voyage of our soul through our personal relationships with others.

Through the ages, many mystics, sages, singers and poets have expressed the ballad and call to love as the ultimate goal. Hunt does the same as he recounts his growing connection with Bunny in his personal wonderland of unconditional love. As he "falls down the Bunny hole" we begin to get a feeling for how living in this world of unconditional love changes his life.

Some years ago I crafted a practical definition for this all-encompassing universal wisdom, simply stated - unconditional love is an unlimited way of being. This explanation removes the limits to our thoughts and feelings, and with it, we can create any reality we choose. The story that unfolds in these pages, and which leads to Hunt's *Relationship Revelations*, is a sparkling example of this.

To say that we absolutely need a special someone to help us on our adventure limits our potential to grow and evolve. However, romantic love can definitely provide a very dynamic way of getting there. Hunt illustrates how once love is triggered in a personal way, it can expand, extending this "unlimited way of being" into our entire world, transforming it into an awe-inspiring wonderland.

The chapter titled, Hunt's Hierarchy of Partnership Priorities spells out exactly how romantic love can lead to an enhanced perspective on life and self actualization. This is summed up in his

Revelation 7: A good relationship gives you confidence in your abilities and helps you stay inspired to do and be your best.

"Love is the magic cookie that makes even the smallest person a giant!"

Some may think it takes extraordinary strength and courage to break free from our past thought forms and limiting beliefs, traumas and dramas, yet Hunt clearly shows us how anyone can awaken their own dreams, find inner peace, and embrace their limitless potential while enjoying the path with another.

This *Introduction* would not be complete without a comment about Hunt's precious awareness and demonstration of unconditional love which is what brought the two us together in the first place. From my somewhat unique vantage point with The Love Foundation, where our vision is "inspiring people to love unconditionally," I am fortunate to interact, learn and grow from individuals of all cultures, races and nations. Hunt knows firsthand that loving unconditionally begins within and by the time you finish his book, you will comprehend this as well.

There are infinite imaginative possibilities when we allow our awareness of freedom to go beyond our normal perceived limits. If we can dream it, we can build it. Life, through unconditional love, is an amazing exploration that excites the very core of our being and lights our path with delight. It is available at any moment by turning our attention to it and Hunt & Bunny's "Adventures in Wonderland" reminds us to do just that.

Harold W. Becker is an author and the President and Founder of the nonprofit, **The Love Foundation,** *www.thelovefoundation.com*

Preface to Peace
by Therese Black

The more I read *Relationship Revelations*, the more I like it!

"We're all in the pits together. ...Incarnating on Earth is all about relationships, and so scaling the pyramid of our personal growth is also dependent upon our relationships." ~from "Hunt's Hierarchy of Partnership Priorities"

The world's population unconsciously cooperates in creating theft, poverty, war, violence... things most of us agree we don't want in our lives. Cooperating to create peace is a little trickier. Still, Hunt's *15 Relationship Revelations* outline how that might be possible.

Relationships and cooperation affect everything from mankind's basic needs to our higher personal and group attainments. As far as I'm concerned, the highest group attainment is peaceful cohabitation in the largest group we have – the One World we all share.

Hunt's simple story illustrates how relationships can possibly operate without the underlying tension that currently describes our world and defines national politics. His relationship revelations are like points on a map that can lead to the treasure of personal satisfaction and world peace.

When you connect the dots, a picture of peace and harmony is revealed. Then, following the path back to its source, we discover from every single angle that the secret starting point begins when we resolve to care about others, all others, as much as we do about ourselves.

This involves overcoming some very natural prejudices. Hunt's message is that it's worth it! His motivation was Bunny. However, if you want harmony at home (wherever you define that to be) try applying his revelations and see if you don't establish possibilities for peace that never existed before.

Hunt provides an excellent, multifaceted perspective on relationships, which can be light or heavy, loving or hateful. This book is a fun reminder that focusing on love not only feels best, but also affords us the best chance of creating the most peace and harmony in of our lives.

"Love can take the heaviest realities and make them light. Love is literally the difference between Heaven and Hell."

This is true for everyone. Even the worst of terrorists, child soldiers, and other dangerous, violent types started life with some degree of love around them. Someone cared enough to feed them and raise them. Somewhere along the way, these people lost their connection to love.

If you think back to your earliest memories, you'll remember instances of how you were raised in love. Also, maybe since then, someone loved you and you loved them. Our lives, and all creation, starts with love. If there were one single prerequisite to peace, caring about your opponent as much as you do yourself would be it.

Two truths regarding love and war were recognized and understood thousands of years ago. Those two truths are here in quotes:

—"Kindness in words creates confidence. Kindness in thinking creates profundity. Kindness in action creates love." ~Lao Tzu

—"Those who go into battle and win will want to go back. Those who lose in battle will want to go back and win." ~Sun Tzu – Ancient Chinese military general, strategist, and philosopher (722–481 BC)

Relationship Revelations reinforces the kindness principle of Lao Tzu and illustrates how that can break the endless cycle Sun Tzu describes.

As you read *Hunt and Bunny's Adventures in Wonderland* you will find your own memories of love and hope reemerging. Connect to those memories, believe in those hopes. For only then can love move in and empower you to build the foundation for peace we all need.

Therese Black is the author of *1 World Peace Plan*
www.thereseblack.com

Relationships are like a dance. They work best when there's just enough resistance to allow you to really feel your partner...

My Intro to Ebony

My first revelation upon meeting Bunny was that **black is not always as different from white as it might seem.** Getting to know her has been like exploring my own soul. Of course, there are differences, but surprisingly, those are the aspects of her that I appreciate most.

Revelation 2: Accepting the differences between ourselves and others broadens our horizons and deepens our soul.

Lots of differences translates to tremendous potential for a broadening that can only be described as the marvelously mystical experience of *Wonderland!* My realization of this wonderland unfolded so quickly that I was afraid that my revelations might slip away if I didn't record them along with my story

Let's begin the story with a quick look at the most obvious difference between Bunny and me. Race should probably be irrelevant in the search for partnership paradise. However, since my exploration took me deep into ebony country, I did a little research to better understand what I was getting into and how our cultural differences might fit into my partnership puzzle.

Interracial marriage was only legalized in all of the United States in 1967, and The Bureau of Statistics chart below shows how very uncommon it is for a white man to marry a black woman:

Married couples in the United States in 2010 (thousands):

	White Wife	Black Wife	Asian Wife	Other Wife
White Husband	50,410	168	529	487

There are many reasons why men may want to date and marry within their same race, or a particular different race for that matter. However, if you simply never considered crossing the racial lines, as was the case with me, I strongly suggest broadening your horizons.

I've been married three times. Also, since my last divorce 14 years ago, I've had a number of relationships, all but one of which were very disappointing. Bunny is the one exception, and she's also the only black woman I've ever dated. Our extreme compatibility could have absolutely nothing to do with her race. Still, it made me wonder...

Bunny has totally changed my life, and although I'm sure that my delight with her is largely individual specific, there are some definite cultural distinctions that many black women share.

The 2011 Census reveals that over 47% of the African-American women over the age of 15 in the U.S. never married. That's almost half of them! By comparison, only 24% of the white women over the age of 15 in the U.S. never married.

So, black women are almost twice as likely to never marry as white women in the U.S., which raises many important questions. However, from the limited viewpoint of a guy looking for a girl, this fact might also infer that many marriage-minded black women are going to be twice as anxious as their Caucasian counterparts to make a man happy.

Black women are also strong and confident – I suspect from having a historically secure, authoritative place in the family. Many men claim to like the idea of a submissive woman. However, general submissiveness can often be traced to a lack of confidence, and I've found that can often backfire in the form of paranoia about being controlled or not valued enough. A guy will have to go way out of his way to constantly assure them that he values their opinions. During my last few relationships, I was as complimentary as I could be, and I'd word things as carefully as possible, and I was still always getting in trouble.

I have no way of knowing how many of my relationship issues were grounded in the culture of the race I dated. However, now that I consider that possibility, I think that many of them very well could be.

When I met Bunny, many of my painful past lives with other women flashed across my mind. I still review those strained relationships now and then, because it reminds me how very fortunate and grateful I am to have discovered Bunny. It also reminds me to be on guard of all the things that can go wrong.

Once, I relayed the message that a friend thought my former partner was attractive. I thought she'd appreciate hearing that. However, her instant reply was that it was an insulting comment. This is the same woman who went to EST meetings to learn to take responsibility for her life. Then she went to therapy for years learning to undo that training because all that responsibility was just too much. That sophisticated and slippery thinking around responsibility aversion resulted in us never being able to resolve any of our issues.

This occurred right before I met Bunny and was hit with

Revelation #3: The most important relationship technique is to sincerely care about the other person more than your own ego.

The examples of the reverse are fairly infinite, and I think that's part of what makes a really good, giving relationship so rare and valuable. Once, when I was with a different woman, I commented at the end of a movie that I prefer happy endings, and she lectured me for 15–20 minutes on how that's not realistic and blasted me for expecting such nonsense.

Then there was the petite woman I tried to get to know off and on for a couple of years. She and Bunny really are as different as black and white, – day and night, bounty and blight! In the two years we saw each other, we never got intimate. Still, we got close enough at the end that she started to feel some sort of responsibility to me and my daughter. This cooperative relationship translated in her mind to a loss of personal control over her life. So, she began to see me as controlling, and suddenly it was all over.

When I pointed out to her what seemed to have happened as diplomatically as I could, she shouted back, "I am not broken!"

I'd never thought of her that way, nor had I ever thought of anyone as broken beyond repair until that moment. However, after that, my frustration resulted in the conclusion that we're all broken to one degree or another. Perhaps it was all about compatibility and no one's fault. However, that was my perception, and I only mention it to help put my deep appreciation for Bunny in perspective – and to point out that I haven't felt broken anymore ever since I met her.

I didn't meet Bunny until I was in my late fifties. She had been divorced 30 years when we met, which made her, I think, about 32 years old — and she was adorable! She was also totally open and didn't have any of the apprehensions and issues I had come to believe were just part of the modern woman's normal condition.

The fact that Bunny is black really has nothing to do with the theme of this book, which I hope you'll come to think of as guide to that alternative world where everything is based on the foundational principles of love.

Still personally, I've wondered if some of my past relationship challenges may have, at least in part, been based on some specific cultural phenomenon related to the challenges white women have had to deal with throughout modern history.

They fought for the right to vote. Then they fought for equal rights in the workplace. They continue to fight against prejudice in the workplace and for changing roles at home. It's not inconceivable that they've been fighting for their rights so long that it's difficult to change out of the combative mindset.

Men have the same problem changing gears when they come home after fighting at work all day. This world is full of challenges for all of us, and it's sometimes hard to shift out of the adversarial approach to life. Still, we aren't ever going to maintain a happy relationship until we do.

In an attempt to cure the cause of their dysfunctional relationships, many women go to seminars where quasi-spiritual gurus enable them with justification for the lack of love in their lives. Their relationship failures are then magically transformed into the basis of a new lesson about independence. After a few drum beats and ohms, they run home to share their new wisdom with all their girlfriends – on Facebook, in woman's magazines, talk shows... everywhere.

"We're all complete within ourselves," is the basic message, and that statement of the currently accepted conventional wisdom is essentially true. In fact, the truth in it is what makes it so dangerous. We were all put on Earth with other people for a reason, and having a special, intimate partner can have a delightfully unique purpose.

Like many, I've only had limited success with that purpose. Still, it seems to me that we can only go one of two ways: give up on finding an intimate partner and rationalize the heck out of that decision, or keep on trying to be open and honest, and continue to hope to attract a partner that fills us with more joy than all the wise platitudes in the world.

The feeling I've gotten after hearing for years that these women don't need anyone is that many just don't really believe in romantic possibilities anymore, which creates a self-fulfilling prophesy. In the immortal words of Celine Dion, "Love comes to those who believe it, and that's the way it is."

"Love is a fruit in season at all times, and within reach of every hand. ~ Mother Teresa

Also the way it is, is that learning to get along with an intimate partner is valuable (perhaps essential) training to getting along with others in a deeply real and sincere way. Getting along with others is in turn essential training to learning how to get along with everyone, which is basically what's required before we can have peace on earth. So, giving up on the one-on-one foundation of all that, because you think you don't need anyone else, is not only sad on a personal level, but it may have far reaching consequences that are even sadder.

When I tried on numerous occasions to explain to Bunny how many women have been trained to believe that they don't need anyone else in their lives, she couldn't ever relate to that idea. Then she'd explain to me her very traditional understanding of the way love "should be," and that "quiet, still voice" inside me would stand up and shout "YES" every time!

Bunny also isn't nearly as touchy about "losing herself" in a relationship. Perhaps again that's because African American women have traditionally had a respected position in the family, so they don't feel challenged and threatened at every turn.

I've found I can say anything to Bunny, so much so that I'm not even careful anymore. When I say something that's a bit off (as I often do), I just get, "Oh, no, no, no, honey..."

I'm corrected without any personal attack or fault assigned. I love it! I'd almost rather say something that she disagrees with, because it's such a relief to see that

I'm still loved, and because her reaction presents such a stark contrast to my other relationships with all those supposedly enlightened women.

Bunny is confident enough in herself to stand toe to toe without ever questioning the deeper feelings on which the relationship is based. Relationships are like a dance. They work best when there's just enough resistance to allow you to really feel your partner, so you can move as one – which beats the heck out of pushing your partner clumsily around the floor, whether you're the pusher or the pushee.

All women are beautiful in their own way, and with the proper nurturing (from themselves and/or others) they can all be divinely beautiful. Still, I've been particularly impressed by darker skinned women lately. Perhaps it's because of the family values, down-to-earth openness, and the confident attitude of the ones I've met. Or perhaps it could just be because they remind me of Bunny – and of love and happiness, and all that's best in the world.

My Intro to God

"Who in the world am I? Ah, that's the great puzzle."
~ Lewis Carroll, Alice in Wonderland

During the 13 years between the time my last marriage ended and the moment I met Bunny, I tried to convince myself that "we're all complete within ourselves." I grew up thinking that it was romantic to love someone so much that you couldn't live without them. However, as an adult, I found out I was wrong. I was informed by many white women (who had attended a weekend seminar or read an article) that needing anyone was actually a psychological disorder known as co-dependency. Their psychobabble and misapplied spiritual principles condemned most of my romantic notions.

After hearing the same thing many times, I figured something must be wrong with me because I just couldn't get comfortable with the reality they described. The feeling that something was missing continued to grow. I knew I wanted to be loved, but I know now that I didn't really know what that meant. I longed for many things, but I was also getting sadly resolved to certain realities. Then I met Bunny, and it was like stepping into a whole new world.

I suppose it could be described as real intimacy. There's joy; there's constant delight! However, what strikes me deepest is the unspoken (until now I guess) mutual agreement to be vulnerable and sacrifice for each other. I know of several people who would say that the relationship boarders on codependency, because we value the needs of each other so much.

According to Wikipedia, codependency "refers to the dependence on the needs of, or control of another. It also often involves placing a lower priority on one's own needs, while being excessively preoccupied with the needs of others."

So, I suppose the self-sacrificial aspect of our relationship could be contrived to be a psychological disorder. Actually though, although we both know we're "complete in ourselves," we're also discovering the tremendous value of our partnership. Pearl S. Buck once said that, "The person who tries to live alone will not succeed as a human being. His heart withers if it does not answer another heart. His mind shrinks away if he hears only the echoes of his own thoughts and finds no other inspiration. "

I think I've probably met many women who's fear of losing themselves in a relationship has caused them to "not succeed as a human being."

Revelation #4: Learning to care about something bigger than yourself is what growing up is all about.

Learning to get along with a partner teaches us to be a couple. That in turn aids in learning to get along with everyone, which teaches us our place in society and in the body of God.

I think these woman's group gurus have done their patrons a tremendous disservice by oversimplifying some spiritual and psychological principles, so that women give up their innate, divinely instilled desires for love and intimacy. A whole generation, or two or three, of women have evidently gotten comfortable with pulling back their concern and allegiance to numero uno.

Personally, I believe that this prevailing wisdom is a tragic misconception, and I know where my allegiance lies:

"I pledge allegiance to Bunny and to the united state of our relationship—one union under God with reality changing love for all." Amen!

It's not that I don't want to be reasonable; it's just that too much cold, hard logic, especially the selfish kind, can really take the romance out of a romance.

During one of my first conversations with Bunny, I said, "You're wonderful—marry me."

To my surprise, she said, "Okay."

I said, "Wait a minute. One of us has to be the reasonable one."

Instantly, we both said, "Not it."

That was the beginning, and shortly after that, we agreed that one of our wedding vows would have to be to never be reasonable regarding matters of love. Reason will just have to work around our love, and not the other way around.

Bunny reminds me often, "Whatever you want, hunny."

It wasn't that long ago that I dreamed of a time when someone would create an android woman and program her with that line—because real women just don't ever say that! Still, here it was in real life. After the excitement wore off and the realization of the huge heart that originated the statement soaked in, I became inspired me to extend her the same unconditional kindness.

Every time Bunny says, "Whatever you want, hunny," she renews that devotion in me. We don't always agree; we do discuss things. Still, when the discussion has been pretty much exhausted and she still wants me do something, I just do it—because I love her, and she does the same for me.

To me, this feels like a huge responsibility. I don't want to abuse the privilege of her granting me absolutely any and all of my wishes. Still, the arrangement totally delights me, and I remind myself of that when she asks me to do things that I'd rather not do. Usually, what she asks me to do has to do with my health or the happiness of my kids. My requests of her aren't usually nearly as magnanimous.

Regardless, this arrangement reminds us both of the love, which is deepening and becoming more satisfying every day. I think that if couples could trust each other enough to do ANYTHING the other asks, they wouldn't need to remember any other relationship rules. That one rule (do anything your partner asks) puts the entire relationship in a very dynamic, heartfelt balance.

Still, *love* doesn't quite describe the sense of self and purpose that I've found with the help of my accountable partner. When I found Bunny, my discovery of myself was kicked up a notch. I'm not just me anymore. I'm Hunt & Bunny! And that feels suddenly part of something much bigger.

A woman once warned me about giving away too much of myself. Still, I give Bunny everything I have, and she dazzles me by giving me everything she has. This builds me up to much more than I ever was without her. It makes me overflow with gratitude, anxious to also give all I have to all of life. All of life seems to be responding by giving me all that it has in return—and what it has is infinite.

Although *love* may not quite describe the change I've experienced since meeting Bunny, it's the key to making me much more than I ever was before. It's opened my eyes to things that I simply didn't see.

It's made me stronger, and with Bunny as my rudder and the wind in my sails, I'm secure in that strength. I told a woman once that I felt stronger with her, hoping that she felt the same way. Her response: "That's what men say when they want to control you."

Yikes! Cooperation is our biggest tool for making life better for everyone. Yet, there's a whole batch of women who have decapitated that potential because they see a partner as a threat to their self-hood instead of as a means to extend themselves into something bigger and better.

I'm finding a more comfortable and happy place in the world all the time. I'm also getting in touch in a more conscious way with what I can only describe as the loving force that creates order in the universe.

This is an infinite discovery that I'll spend the rest of my life/lives continuing to make. Still, it all started, or maybe was kicked up into a much higher gear, when I started falling for Bunny. It's like I fell down the Bunny hole and landed in Wonderland.

Suddenly, I'm in an entirely different world than I've ever known before. It has its own rules and operates slightly outside the limits of conventional reason. However, once you factor in the soul-satisfying, chaos organizing, power of love, it all makes sense—sort of.

Once I started falling, I never looked back. I surrendered to the womb surrounded by black.

Falling Down the Bunny Hole

"In another moment down went Alice ...
never once considering how in the world she
was to get out again."

~ Lewis Carroll, Alice's Adventures in Wonderland

It all started during a curious moment when I had decided to try out an online dating site. I was doing a search of local women when I noticed that they were flashing the most attractive women from all over the U.S. to the right of my search data. Of course Bunny made the cut, and they made it so easy to send a flirt, that I couldn't resist. From that moment on, life became, as Lewis Carroll put it, "curiouser and curiouser."

I live in Montana and Bunny's in Memphis, so I never expected to meet her, and I thought she would be thinking the same thing. Still, she wrote back to say thank you for my automatic system-generated note, catching my attention and inspiring me to read her profile.

I had seen so many pictures and profiles in rapid succession that I started characterizing all of the women by a one-line statement, a sort of summary message that jumped out at me when I looked at their files. The message I got from Bunny's picture and profile was so unique and surprising that I decided to tell her about it. Why not? I was never going to actually meet this black woman who lived halfway across the country anyway.

I expected that what I was about to say would be taken as an inappropriate sexual comment, and that I'd never hear from her again. Still, it felt like such a powerful message that I decided, what the heck!

So, referring to the women on the site, here's what I wrote her:

"... I tend to summarize them in a one-line statement. When I think of their picture, that statement comes to my mind (instead of a name). The statement that summarizes one woman on this site is: *I don't know what I want anymore, but I need hugs.* The message I get from another particularly pretty woman is *I'm fine alone, but go ahead and try to talk to me if you want.* One is simply into cowboy fantasies, and what I hear behind everything she says is, *Let's play.* That's it, and I don't see it going anywhere, but it' could be sort of fun I guess.

"You stand out as THE most solid, real-person potential—even tho there's no real possibility we'll be getting together because of the distance and other differences between us. Still, when I think of you, the message I get is *I'll take care of you. No problem.*

"Wow. I had to go back a few times to confirm that message, but that's what I keep getting. You're solid, strong, grounded, and you'll take care of your partner in every possible way—"no problem.""

"That approach to a relationship will put everything in order. Priorities like fun and family, life and purpose, building something together that you can leave to your posterity, and values you'll convey to them will all fall into place."

I said a few more strange things that I had no business saying that day (October 23, 2012) too. Still, by the end of it, Bunny says now that she was convinced that I was "the one." It was soon after that that she started saying, "Whatever you want, hunny," and my free-fall began.

I fell happily down that Bunny hole, trusting somehow that the landing would be soft. After chatting with Bunny a couple of days, I bought tickets to fly out to see her a couple of weeks later on the Thanksgiving weekend. I felt surprising comfortable (although very white) surrounded by all of her family that weekend. However, at this writing, I'm still falling and we're both looking forward to being grateful next Thanksgiving for the anniversary of our first date.

Bunny came out to see me a month later after Christmas. We spent a few days at the Hot Springs, and we took many private baths together. As with my Thanksgiving experience, I was surprisingly comfortable with her – sitting in the healing waters together just talking, relaxing and smiling a lot at each other. It was like I'd been with this woman my whole life.

I proposed at the end of our Hot Springs trip and sent her home with a ring. Still, the plan to be with each other forever hasn't made it any easier to catch my footing. Even as I'm very aware of landing in Wonderland, I'm still very conscious of continuing to fall deeper down the hole – not just deeper in love, but also deeper into uncharted territory.

Waking in Wonderland

"We're all mad here. I'm mad. You're mad"

~ Lewis Carroll, Alice in Wonderland

When I first landed in wonderland, I was like a kid who could have anything he wanted in a candy shop. I was delighted and excited! It was the first day of vacation from school. Colors were brighter. Sounds were clearer, and smells were more enticing, and I felt deeply blissful.

I hoped I hadn't gone mad, but that possibility did cross my mind. I wanted to trust the bliss, but I was a little concerned that Bunny was all I could ever think about.

I see nothing but you.
I hear nothing but you.
I am nothing but you.
~ Sri Gawn Tu Fahr

I think that may be going a bit tu fahr. I wasn't quite ready to admit that I was nothing without her, but I was beginning to get worried that I might be getting a little over-committed too quickly. Still, being close to Bunny made my heart peaceful and quieted my anxiety. Talking to her reminded me that I'm not alone anymore. All the world was suddenly my friend and family. Hugging her reminded me that I'm blessed with my own personal connection to the divine. Going to sleep with her, and waking up next to her, renewed my faith in Wonderland—every day and every night.

I tried to discern when the feast might end and the everyday sustenance might begin. I whined to myself as I wondered why that has to happen, secretly hoping that if the love is strong enough that the narcotic of newness might never wear off.

Reality hit when Bunny casually admitted that she was actually a couple years older than I was previously led to believe.

It was a small thing. Still, my bubble of bliss popped as all the times I felt manipulated and betrayed at the end of my previous relationships flashed across my mind. My boat had been torpedoed, and it quickly sank.

However, it resurfaced when I remembered all the things I love about Bunny. Of course, I still want to be with her forever. This was one little test, and there'll be others. Bring 'em on!

In the end, real love had only been tempered by the fire of my exploding illusion and the water that had initially swamped me. It was a little sad when I stopped floating on clouds, but it also feels good to finally have a firmer footing in Wonderland. The dream was nice, but waking and realizing that I can still stay in this wondrous place is better.

Wonderland is the way I always thought relationships should be—giving and forgiving and full of peaceful endings and happy beginnings. Because here, love conquers all!

Revelation 5: Love has a life all its own that is more important than any individual life involved.

It has a logic that goes beyond enlightened self-interest. It has a mystical quality that creates harmony in everything it touches, and it's a shame that's not better recognized.

Lewis Carroll: "We're all mad here."

Bunny: "We have what others don't believe in."

The 18th Century Irish poet, Thomas Moore, stated what is still probably the conventional wisdom on the subject: "Romantic love is an illusion. Most of us discover this truth at the end of a love affair or else when the sweet emotions of love lead us into marriage and then turn down their flames"

To this Bunny said, "I don't believe that. Love makes the world go around!" She makes everything so simple, and her conviction can be contagious.

Also, I just can't imagine that all the songs and stories and obsessions about love that saturate the media could all be based on mere illusion. There must be something to it! There must be some key to the wonderland of enduring love that the beautiful people know how to use intuitively and that is so baffling to the profane that they write off that pervasive myth as pure illusion.

Now that I've woken up in Wonderland, I know there is more to it than illusion. It's a total life-changer, and I think everyone should give the romantic world down the bunny hole a chance!

"Take the red pill—you stay in Wonderland, and I show you just how deep the rabbit hole goes..." from *The Matrix*

The difference between Wonderland and The Matrix though is that, despite the claims of some to the contrary, we aren't just exploring an illusionary world here. Although romance can be fragile and needs protecting, the goal is to find out just how deep it can go and what sort of wonderland marvels it will lead to.

Think of love as a camp fire. I love to build fires so huge that you can't even get very close to them. That's an amazing sight and a wonderful feeling—just like new love.

However, you can't cook on it until the flames have died down and you have some stable coals. Look for the stable coals in your romantic partner, and then feed them so they always glow warm and bright, so that you both can get fed.

When Bunny got back to work with her engagement ring, she was told that she was glowing. Yet, in the days that passed with her there and me thousands of miles away, our glow started to dim until we realized what was happening, talked, and got that happy warmth rekindled.

Physical touch puts everything in order, but in Wonderland, it's not absolutely necessary. Nothing is necessary but love and genuine concern. Bunny's body may be far away, but her essence has taken up residence in my heart. I feel it in a very real, palpable way. One morning, I was woken up out of a deep sleep by her voice. Although she was physically half the country away, I heard her say, "Hunny," so loud and clear that I sat straight up in bed looking for her. Turns out she was playing a little game to see if she could connect with me. However, even without the strange connections, she still regularly reminds me of her love on the phone and emails, so she's always with me.

Remember, in this special mindset we're calling Wonderland, love conquers all. Love is more powerful than distance, differences, and even the disdain and the damning prejudice of the outside world.

Still, keeping those coals red hot week after week, month after month, year after year takes diligence. It's not really work because it's a labor of love. Still, if you get distracted for too long, you'll come back to find your home fires reduced to nothing but a pile of dead ashes. No one wants that. So tend those fires. You know how!

I was told once that if something bad happens in a relationship, you need at least five good things to balance it out. Reminding each other of your love in lots of little ways can become a wonderful way of life. It's easy to think things are fine, but then you slip out of that way of life and when one or two little bad things happen, it can be devastating.

To this situation, Alfred, Lord Tennyson offers us this consolation: "*Tis better to have loved and lost than never to have loved at all.*"

However, why does love have to be lost so often? Having adequate desire and commitment to feed the fire of your relationship is a big part of it. Still, desire and commitment are themselves fed by the knowledge of what you have in your partner. I've only been with Bunny for a relatively short while, but I'm very conscious of how much better she is than any woman I've ever known. The comparisons are so outlandish that the knowledge of what I have in her jumps out at me constantly, making me very motivated to endure our long distance relationship as long as necessary and to do all I can to keep her happy.

I'm afraid that the knowledge of what many have in their partner grows a bit hazy over time, so it can't support their best intentions the way it should. I'm no relationship expert, but as Bob Dylan said, "You don't need to be a weatherman to know which way the wind blows."

Common sense dictates that you remind yourself daily about what you love about your partner to keep those thoughts fresh and vital. What does he or she do for you? What needs do they fill? See if you can think that through and list exactly why you love your special friend.

There are many reasons to appreciate your mate and many needs that you can fill for each other. There is also a natural hierarchy to prioritizing those needs that no one has ever addressed the way I do in the next chapter. I believe that's because relationship needs can appear to be as diverse as the individuals involved. Also, the job of psychologists is generally to help their patients find emotional balance and become better functioning in society. What I'm preaching is entirely different.

A balanced and functional life is just the beginning.

Revelation 6: The goal of carefully and faithfully applying the transformational power of love results in nothing short of life liberating, soul satisfying salvation!

Hallelujah and Geronimo! Jumping down that infinitely deep Bunny hole may seem like quite a leap of faith, but I'll be breaking it down for you. The bottom-line key to reaching this Heaven, and not being booted out of romance wonderland on your way, is to satisfy your partners needs on increasingly subtle levels, while they do the same for you.

It's a matter of simple cooperation. Still, it's not so simple that just anyone can do it. Love has to become more important than many of your ideas, inclinations or ego. However, for those who can pass that test, the pearly gates to the land of unlimited potential are flung wide open!

Love may be fragile, but when nurtured, it can also be delightfully durable. Relationships can last! It is possible to continually be rewarded and challenged as you pursue the on-going adventure of learning who you are and what you want to do together with your partner. I don't see any reason the special sense of a life mission together should ever fade, or that a couple should ever tire of the endless possibilities of exploring their shared existence. A loving relationship has the power to be more significant to every aspect of your life than you'd probably ever imagine. I'll tell you exactly how and why in a few more pages.

For now, just plan on being relieved and let yourself indulge the hopes for happiness that you used to expect out of life. Also, plan on taking the time to take care of your partner's needs, because when you do, romantic love becomes a sort of elevator that carries you up the pyramid of your potential.

Hunt's Hierarchy of Partnership Priorities

"How puzzling all these changes are! I'm never sure what I'm going to be, from one minute to another."

~ Lewis Carroll, Alice's Adventures in Wonderland

In this world where "one pill makes you larger and one pill makes you small, it's hard to know what you're going to be from one minute to the next – at all!"

~Hunt

"When logic and proportion have fallen sloppy dead... remember what the Dormouse said, "Feed your head..."

~Jefferson Airplane, from White Rabbit

Let's begin the feeding with a little story. One of the things I said to Bunny (the first day we met) was that I wanted to be accountable to someone I trusted, so I could start to get a better grip on "logic and proportion."

I told her I wanted someone to inspire me and gently hold me to my highest intentions. I quickly found out that she wanted that too. Yet, because that desire is fairly high on the hierarchy of needs pyramid, it's not usually something people talk about.

For some reason, people don't generally talk about their highest or lowest needs. The highest ones are often irrelevant until you get the lower ones satisfied -- and because the lower ones are rarely adequately satisfied, those higher ones just aren't usually thought about very much by most people.

Also, the human needs toward the bottom of the pyramid (like sex) are generally considered impolite to discuss. So, what people tell each other they want out of a relationship are usually the safe ones in the middle of the needs hierarchy: "I like dancing and taking long walks on the beach."

That may not actually address your real immediate concerns, and it doesn't really touch the higher ones either. Those walks on the beach may lead to sex, but without understanding and cooperating with your partner on all of your needs, passion from those walks on the beach eventually grows cold, and you find yourself looking for someone else to walk with hand-in-hand into the sunset, all the time wondering what went wrong.

What went wrong was that neither partner had an adequate grasp of all the things they needed from each other, nor any idea of how to go about fulfilling all those needs that are a bit more elusive than sex and companionship.

Finally, here it is: **the definitive answer to achieving blissful partnership harmony and personal growth – according to Hunt.**

When I ran this chapter by a psychiatrist I know, she wrote back with pages of suggestions on how to add "meat" to my skeleton of the partnership hierarchy in order to make this chapter into a serious piece of work. My reaction was to go the other way, and make it even less serious than it was already. I'm purposefully oversimplifing some very complicated and convoluted considerations in hopes of revealing a big picture that often gets lost in all the emotional and mind-numbing confusion of partnership dynamics.

Disclaimer: I'm not a psychiatrist and I fully realize that I'm far from the perfect example of a person who has applied any of this. I expect that if I personally inspire anyone, it will be because they'll be thinking, "If he can do it, then I sure can!"

It was, in fact, a lifetime of relationship conflict and anguishing self-analysis that drove me to put this all together, and I couldn't have done it without the insightful help of others. In laying this all out, I'm not putting myself above ANYONE. We're all in the pits together. It's just that I think I see the way out, and my main point is that we can do it by cooperating with each other. Incarnating on Earth is all about relationships, and so scaling the pyramid of our personal growth is also dependent upon our relationships.

In 1943, an American psychologist by the name of Abraham Maslow described the progress towards psychological health in terms of the fulfillment of innate human needs in sequence, from the lowest to the highest, eventually culminating in what he called *self-actualization*. According to Maslow, the highest needs couldn't generally be fulfilled until the lower ones were satisfied to some degree. You can see why it works this way by looking at his descriptions of our human needs.

Maslow's Hierarchy

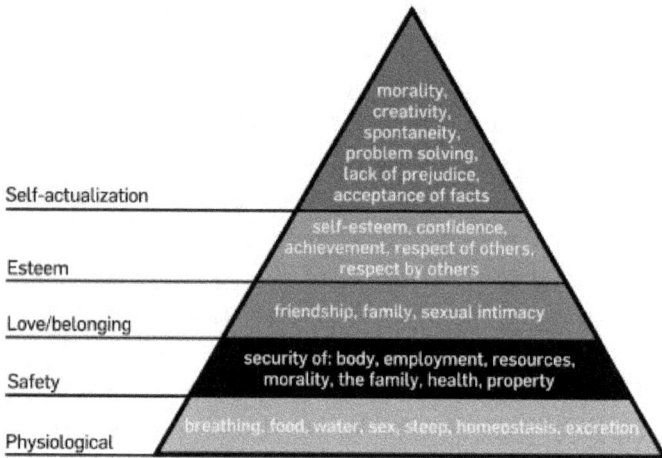

Maslow never actually suggested how to go about fulfilling those needs. He just stated what they are and observed that the highest ones are unachievable until the lower needs are handled.

In the Western society, we tend to think we need to do everything alone. Our philosophical Greek heritage dictates the importance of individualism and personal achievement. However, with feelings of isolation, suicide rates and anti-depressant usage at all-time highs, it might be time to start thinking about how our relationships might help us scale this pyramid.

To help you think that through, I've constructed my own pyramid – a partnership pyramid. And I'll explain how scaling it with a partner helps us to achieve our higher goals as laid out by Maslow.

Hunt's Hierarchy

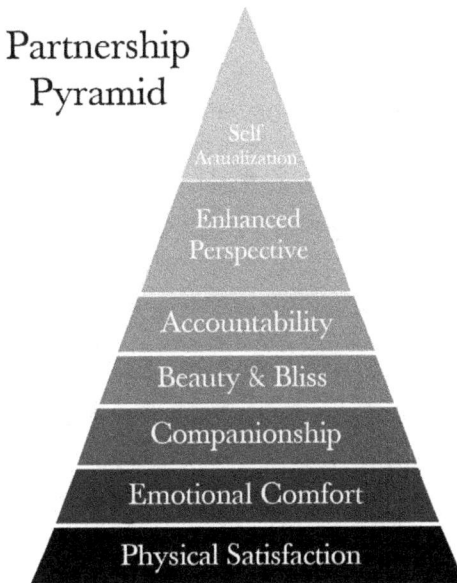

Partnership Pyramid

Self Actualization

Enhanced Perspective

Accountability

Beauty & Bliss

Companionship

Emotional Comfort

Physical Satisfaction

Just like there are seven wonders in the world and seven primary chakras in our body, I figure our relationship needs also break down to seven basic levels.

Physical satisfaction includes human touch. Babies have been known to die without it. Many of us have gone through times where we feel we're dying too – a good indication that physical touch and regular hugs are pretty important. Intimacy with your partner is important on all levels, but it's easiest to talk about on the lower ones. They say men give emotional intimacy to get physical intimacy, and it's the other way around for women.

It's been my experience that men and women are "the other way around" from each other on many issues. But then, that's probably at the core of the reason we need each other. The opposite sex can help us achieve balance by providing a complementary perspective that can be great training for all of our relationships.

Also, since physical and emotional intimacy is so important, the desire to keep it in our lives helps us stay motivated to get along with our partner and stay the course as we climb the pyramid. You might say that intimacy is the glue that holds a relationship together.

It can also help us hold our individual self together. Personally, I've found that when I'm not in a relationship, I drink more and care less – about everything.

I suppose it's possible to live a well-balanced life in abstinence.

However, our physical bodies have needs that affect our emotions and minds, and they need to be handled one way or another.

Perhaps sensuality and sexuality isn't absolutely necessary in order to take care of your lower needs. However, I personally believe that a partner of some sort is required to help us keep our footing on the higher levels of the pyramid. And since we need one for that, it just makes sense to try to interest them in those lower steps too -- which would make getting what we need on those lower levels much more satisfying are easier.

Emotional Comfort can verify that our physical needs are being met (especially if you happen to be of the male persuasion). However, I've been assured by my psychiatrist friend that it really is a stand-alone need. Maslow sums up a lot of this need in his level three, which includes the comfort we derive from family, friends, sexual intimacy, and a sense of belonging. It's this "sense of belonging" that's key to our emotional comfort, and that brings us back to our relationships. Whether or not we have a special someone in our lives, we need to be grounded in relationships to the point that we're comfortable enough with life to take that next step up the pyramid of personal growth.

Companionship requires a personal relationship with someone, and I see it as as specialized enhancement to general emotional comfort that we can obtain through our "sense of belonging" to one group or another. When people say they want someone to go dancing with or to accompany them on long walks, they're looking to fulfill their need for companionship, so they don't "feel alone." Because even if you have a sense of belonging, you can still feel alone unless your companionship needs are filled. Still, this is probably the easiest level for everyone to relate to and the least threatening.

Taking further steps up the pyramid with a partner becomes increasingly threatening to many! I tried to date a woman once who ended up deciding she didn't need anyone special in her life because she had all her girlfriends. At that point, she had decided to not progress any further up the partnership pyramid. She needed to rest on the companionship level for a while in order to make herself feel safe. Notice where safety is on Maslow's pyramid (level two.)

Bunny and I like to assume that when our kids and others look at us, they'll imagine us having pleasant conversation over tea – and staying at the companionship level. Everyone knows there's a whole hierarchy of needs that couples help each other with, but no one really wants to think about it. It's a little threatening to their ideas and images of the way things "should be."

Beauty and bliss is the first step into the subtle levels of our human experience. That means that although everyone has the need, they just don't think about it much – at least as much as they do about comfort and companionship. Still, when you stare at a flower or bird or a beautiful woman a little longer than necessary to acknowledge the physical object in front of you, you're engaging your appreciation of beauty, and a state of bliss (to some degree) is the eventual result.

That's because as the beauty soaks in, everything around you begins to look more beautiful. At those times, a sense of the order in the universe will captivate my attention. Bliss has been described as ecstasy and rapture. Still, as those particular manifestations of the bliss consciousness fade, the joy and serene confidence in life that bliss instills remains. That joy and confidence then becomes footholds to help you scale the pyramid further from that level.

As you might imagine, you can find beauty everywhere and bliss can result from many different peak experiences that result from your engagement with that beauty. However, the point is that relationships are key, and having a special someone capable of regularly stimulating your bliss is a tremendous blessing that I don't think anyone should ever give up on entirely.

Comfort and companionship make us emotionally stable and strong. Beauty and bliss makes us confident. Then, *accountability* makes us dependable.

Again, this is an oversimplification. Still, I think it's a useful one. If you don't look too closely, and just stand back and take in the big picture, it's easy to see how a partner can play an important role in our psychological health and personal growth.

Accountability is the first step that describes our use of our partnership in a way that's not primarily self-serving. At this level, we apply the love of life we've generated at the other levels to our responsibilities and pursuits. This is where we take our first steps on the illusive path of finding purpose and eventually self-actualization.

Accountability denotes that you're held responsible for doing your best. So, in order to really work at this level, you'll need an accountable partner to

- hold you to your highest intentions, and inspire you,

- discuss your slip-ups in a gentle and loving way, and

- help you achieve a more consistently constructive perspective on life.

Granted, some need this external input much more than others. Still, we all need it to some degree. An accountable partner doesn't need to be a sexual partner, but it does need to be someone you love, so that you're motivated to remain being accountable to them. Someone who is also intimately involved, concerned, and accountable to you makes the perfect partner for this purpose. A child fulfills part of that requirement because of your love for, and accountability to, that child. However, an accountable partner also needs to be someone who will give you reliable feedback on how well you're living up to the responsibilities that your love initiated.

"It is good to have an end to journey toward; but it is the journey that matters, in the end." ~ Ernest Hemingway

Having two different people for these two different roles (someone to love and be accountable to and a different person to tell you how you're doing in with those responsibilities) doesn't quiet accomplish the same thing. If you aren't really responsible for someone, their input will never be as reliable as someone who is affected by your decisions and actions. Their advice may be easier to hear, but it will never be as useful as if it came from a truly accountable partner.

However, having a *partner of consequence* with whom you share all your thoughts is the next best thing. If both partners are completely honest with each other, that relationship can create a sense of accountability even though your living conditions don't forcibly impose that condition.

Your accountable partner's job is to acknowledge when you live up to your responsibility of making their life better than it would be without you, and when you don't. They also should be able to offer valuable insight on how you're living up to your other responsibilities. Ideally, that should go both ways, so both partners serve the same function for each other. That creates balance.

Revelation 7: A good relationship gives you confidence in your abilities and helps you stay inspired to do and be your best.

It also allows you to take one more step up the pyramid to where you have a higher and better perspective on life.

This higher, **enhanced perspective** is made possible because

> **1.** You're learning to base your decisions and actions on love for something greater than yourself; and

> **2.** Because you have another perspective to give your own view of things depth. Just like depth perception isn't possible with only one eye, a sustainable, balanced view of things isn't possible to maintain indefinitely without the help of your accountable partner. Although having a partner to enhanse your perspective doesn't guarantee your personal view point will improve significantly, not having one pretty much assures that it won't.

From this enhanced perspective all of your other fulfilled needs take on new meaning. Sex, comfort, companionship, beauty and bliss all radiate with new life and significance. You also appreciate your trusted, accountable partner with new intensity and understanding. You deeply appreciate everything and everyone that helped you meet all your needs and get you to this level.

This is where "unconditional love" enters in. Love may not always be totally unconditional no matter how much you have to be grateful for. Still, a loving appreciation does make us all better people than we would be otherwise. This does eventually lead to unconditional love, which is part of our evolutionary process. In other words, sooner or later, it's required, because face it: anything else really isn't *love*.

*No wise fish would go anywhere
without a porpoise. ~ Lewis Carroll*

Once your enhanced perspective has settled in, you're ready to move on to what Maslow has called **Self-actualization.** This may be the top of this pyramid, but it's actually just the beginning of your life as a purpose directed human. Just like you need to sleep and eat before you go to work in the morning, you need to walk up the six steps up the partnership pyramid before you're ready to begin your life's work with the proficiency that comes from being secure in the knowledge of who you truly are.

As Carl Jung once put it, "The privilege of a lifetime is to become who you truly are."

This realization of who you truly are (that results largely from the nurturing and constructive feedback of your accountable partner) is your key to actualizing your highest potential, which becomes your new way of life. Goals may change, and successes may not always be apparent, but joy and confidence comes from knowing that your path for expressing yourself in this world is finally secure.

Maslow once wrote that "What a man can be, he must be." In other words, there are natural internal forces that drive us up through the hierarchy of needs if we, individually and as a society, cooperate with those urges. Unfortunately, society has traditionally afforded few with the opportunity to rise above their lower needs. Also, many of those who do have the opportunity to reach their full potential don't recognize it, or understand themselves well enough, to make the most of the opportunity, and that's another reason we need a helping hand from a partner of consequence.

To recognize and achieve our full potential, we also need to somehow master all of our lower needs, so that they don't pull us down and away from our higher pursuits.

Love for another can grow to a love for the whole, after our personal needs are handled. As we rise through the levels of the partnership hierarchy pyramid, often experiencing compatibility challenges, it's good to remember that before we can get along with the world in an honest, satisfying, and sustainable way, we need to master getting along with our partner. Also, a loving, accountable partner may actually be the only sustainable way to see clearly and achieve the enhanced perspective that gives life as much purpose as possible.

Here's an easy way to remember all that: *No wise fish would go anywhere without a porpoise. ~ Lewis Carroll*

One more thing: No discussion of the relationship hierarchy would be complete without at least mentioning our relationship to the spiritual hierarchy. For most people, knowledge of anything or anyone beyond this physical world is mostly irrelevant. However, true, selfless, spiritual love tends to make it increasingly more relevant.

I believe that **angels and guides work with all of us** to help us accomplish what we personally need to while we're still in this world. However, I was told that the guides in the heavenly hierarchy who are in charge of shaping the events of the world don't really work with lone individuals much. They work with groups, and the smallest group they'll work with is a couple who are accountable to each other. Solitary individuals are evidently just too vulnerable to mood and decision swings to be dependable enough to warrant much of their time.

That's just another reason to follow your heart and find someone with whom you can be totally honest about everything. Relationships come in all varieties and colors. Many people have some strong feelings about what's right and what's not. As far as I'm concerned, if it's not covered in my discussion above, it's not universally important. Things like race and gender preference are details best left to the individual.

All that really matters is that we express love, share it, learn from it, grow because of it, and form deep (sometimes intimate) partnerships around it. As anyone in Wonderland will tell you, *love is the most powerful force in the universe.* It can, of course, be used by both males and females. Still, these nurturing relationships, that move us up the partnership pyramid, are all powered by what many call the divine feminine force. And in Wonderland, this intuitive, cooperative, beautifully blissful side of love is the law of the land.

The Divine Feminine Force

"It is not how much we do, but how much
love we put in the doing.
It is not how much we give, but how much
love we put in the giving."
~Mother Teresa

As I mentioned before, whenever Bunny asks me to do something, I just do it. This reminds me that my life is now influenced by something more powerful and divine than just my own mind – or her's for that matter.

"Have I gone mad?"

"I'm afraid so, but let me tell you something. The best people usually are." ~ Lewis Carroll, from *Alice in Wonderland*

It may not be reasonable (or even sane) in conventional terms, but I do my best to surrender to the voice of my heart, which comes from an entirely different place than the whims of my emotions. Love is a good way to tell the difference. And when we put love into everything we do, as Mother T suggests, we're dead center on the path of the divine feminine.

This control Bunny has over me is a tremendous responsibility for her, but it's also how we learn to work closer on the accountability level of the partnership pyramid.

Incidentally, Bunny trusts me a lot too, and we're both getting more trustworthy as we rely on our heart's connection to a higher intelligence to guide us. Bunny refers to this higher force as God.

I see it more as the mind of the universal divine feminine force, and I like to think of it as a beautiful feminine face and voice that I'd follow anywhere.

I suppose that's one version of God. I think what's important about this intelligent force though is how it guides us to have a trusting attitude and to use our intuitive knowing. It inspires a nurturing spirit, and a gentle motherly concern for all of God's children. This spirit is in all of us, but they call it the divine "feminine" for a reason. I think women are primarily the ones responsible for bringing it into this world, and they do seem to be having a louder voice these days.

Some state governments, like Arizona, are currently completely in the hands of women. Recently, the United States almost had a female president for the first time in history. And a good number of countries, maybe over half, have already made the switch to a female head of state.

Here is just a partial list: Mongolia, Argentina, Bolivia, People's Republic of China, Malta, San Marino, Iceland, Switzerland, Philippines, East Germany, Nicaragua, Ireland, Sri Lanka, Liberia, Ecuador, Panama, Finland, Indonesia, Chili, Brazil, Israel, Costa Rica, South Korea, and Lithuania.

Females are increasingly working their ways into leadership roles in business, government, and families. Personally, I think hooking up with a strong black woman fits right into this new order.

Males have controlled the world for about 13,000 years now. However, suddenly that's changing. Not all women are up to the challenge, but many are, and that's essential right now. Personally, I'm beginning to think that if enough women don't step up to their role of introducing a softer, more nurturing attitude into the mainstream, we're friggin' doomed. However, when they do... Wonderland – the promised "Golden Age."

What's the saying? "If women ran the world, no one's sons would ever go to war."

So, after thousands of years of war, we're handing off the torch. Or maybe it will be wrestled out of our hands. Transitions can be messy. However women come into their new roles of authority, it's essential that they also come into an understanding of their divine feminine nature.

In this violent and noisy world, the divine feminine is the peaceful sound of harmony—or of silence.

When I am silent, I fall into the place where everything is music. ♥ Rumi

It's in the sound of children laughing and playing without fear. It's the voice of understanding and concern. Bunny is my living example of the divine feminine. Her love and concern defines her. She's my teacher and inspiration.

My heart stretches every day to try to keep up with her deepening love and devotion. When I wonder about the reason for life, I don't need to look any further than the face of the divine feminine force in front of me, nor do I feel there could be any teaching more important than the lessons of love.

Love is patient, love is kind. It does not envy, it does not boast, it is not proud. It is not rude, it is not self-seeking, it is not easily angered, it keeps no record of wrongs. Love does not delight in evil but rejoices with the truth. It always protects, always trusts, always hopes, always perseveres. Love never fails. ~ 1 Corinthians 13:4–8a (NIV)

What else do we need to know? What else besides learning to defer to this divine feminine wisdom could possibly be required to turn all of life into a wonderland where "love never fails?"

When we allow the heart and its divine feminine guardians to run our lives, we're filled with unconditional love, compassion and understanding, helpfulness toward others, tenderness, and kindness.

Revelation 8: When the feminine force is allowed to fill the minds of men, our worlds don't crash when they collide anymore. They bounce with joy, and everyone celebrates the miraculous reunion.

When Worlds Collide

"What a strange world we live in...Said Alice to the
queen of hearts"

~Lewis Carroll, Alice in Wonderland

The first night I spent with my Queen of Hearts,
she wanted a little time alone in the bedroom, so I
obliged. However, I evidently came in too early, because
I found her still kneeling by the bed saying her prayers.

I haven't been a traditional Christian since I was 12
when I met with my minister to discuss the Christian
beliefs that I knew to be wrong. I was initiated into
Transcendental Meditation when I was in high school. I
practiced Buddhism for several years. I was in Eckankar,
"the religion of the light and sound of God" for over
20 years and served as a member of their clergy for six
years. So, when I met Bunny, I was about as far from
her traditional Christian beliefs as possible. In fact, we
were worlds apart!

Still, did I do to her what Hitler did to the Jews, or

what the Catholics did to everybody, or what the Israelis do to the Arabs and Palestinians, or what capitalists do to communists? Not quite.

When I saw her praying on her knees, my heart melted. I felt her purity and sincerity, and I was more impressed with her than ever. We come from totally different worlds, but somehow, I get along with her better than anyone I've ever known.

When Alice fell down the rabbit hole, her world of Victorian virtue, order, and manners collided with rude characters who challenged her at every turn. She was first taken aback when the White Rabbit mistook her for a servant. The Mad Hatter and the March Hare assaulted her with a seemingly nonsensical logic. Still, what they said somehow seemed consistent with everything else in that strange land. So although Alice suffers a bit of an identity crisis, she moves through Wonderland with a degree of dignity and fits in the best she can.

She constantly encounters puzzles that don't seem to have any solution. Also, her curiosity about how things work in Wonderland sets her apart from everyone else. (Does any of this feel familiar yet?) Eventually, she gives up on trying to make sense out of things. Alice learns to just accept the world the way she finds it, and she seems to discover a little peace in the process.

I can translate the things Bunny says so they make sense to me, and she seems to do the same with me. Still, some things about her world may always baffle me. For instance, knowing my background and beliefs, she still gave me a cross to wear early on. When I asked why, she said she felt guided to get it for me. Instantly I could see someone smiling down at us, and I figured it was a test of our colliding worlds. However, it was given in love, so I wear it for the same reason, and I just try not to think about it too much.

Some things make sense to me. I just accept other things, because when worlds collide, that's just what you do—if you want to stay in Wonderland.

Things work delightfully different here. Sometimes, Bunny misses me so badly that I feel relieved, because somehow that means that I don't have to feel so bad about missing her. Emotions are shared, and we tend to balance each other out. Sometimes, she takes on the bulk of the burden of our separation. Other times I do.

I learned instantly to appreciate the religious life as she sees it. And Bunny began hearing answers to her prayers and seeing her guides shortly after meeting me. When our worlds collided, we were both challenged tremendously. Still, we quickly realized that we were being initiated into a totally new and better world.

For instance, Bunny loves to listen to love songs, and she's really big on black artists. Mostly, I've learned to appreciate the female vocalists – I think partly because they remind me of Bunny. However, usually, whenever I hear the black male vocalists, I'm thinking, "OH NO....Stop!"

I'm not sure why I can't relate, and I feel kind-of bad and confused, but Bunny just laughs it off. *Love is patient, love is kind...*

We were sending each other links to music we liked for a while. Then when she stopped, I stopped. Then she asked why I stopped?

Bunny likes it when I send her love songs, and we agreed that I need to do it at least once a week. And so our colliding worlds continue to "bounce with joy."

You're thinking about something, my dear, and that makes you forget to talk. I can't tell you just now what the moral of that is, but I shall remember it in a bit."

Perhaps it hasn't one, Alice ventured to remark.

Tut, tut, child! said the Duchess. Everything's got a moral, if only you can find it.

~ Lewis Carroll, Alice in Wonderland

One possible moral (from the Mad Hunter):

Revelation 9: Despite how religiously many hang onto their beliefs, the deepest beliefs are still only skin-deep compared to the love for all that's rooted in our infinite source.

The best creations result from the union of opposites (men and women, left brain and right brain, etc.), and our beliefs need to be flexible enough to allow this miracle to happen. So if you're ever fortunate enough to fall down a bunny hole, choose wisely. What you know to be wrong may not be quite as wrong as you thought, and your acceptance may just unlock a miraculous new world.

Romancing Reality

"But, said Alice, the world has absolutely no sense."
"Who's stopping us from inventing one?"

~Lewis Carroll, Alice in Wonderland

Sad realities fill the world. It can be a place of despair and depression, hatred, anger, loathing, and all the other difficult realities you know all too well. Still, you stand your ground, doing your best – even as a new painful realization takes up residence in the back of your mind: Every brave decision and sad resolution you've made secures another lock on the gate between you and Wonderland. You know what's real! And yet, one day, desperate to capture a little beauty for your bare table, you reach through the Wonderland gate to grasp a handful of the flowers of fantasy.

Then gradually, a totally unrealistic hope captivates you. Suddenly, you know beyond any doubt, that you simply have to find a way through, over, or around that gate – to where the world makes a much happier sense.

Love IS Wonderland, and sometimes romance is what it takes to jump-start our sense of a better sense. So in that sense, romance isn't just realistic; it's necessary!

Wonderland may be a step or two off the beaten path. Yet, the path most taken often leads in circles and suffocates us with a stifling reality. Sometimes the only way off that merry-go-round is to take a leap of faith. Pretend that love is around every corner. Pretend that you're walking into Wonderland and see what happens.

"Acting as if" is a fun metaphysical principle that works in the real world whether we believe it or not. We all want to be real. Still, when you act as if you're happy (for instance) long enough, real happiness creeps up on you. When you forget what you know about your limitations, and act as if you can do anything, it's amazing what you can accomplish.

> *"Why, sometimes I've believed as many as six impossible things before breakfast."*
> *~Lewis Carroll, Alice in Wonderland*

Once, when Bunny and I were discussing living arrangements and our separate responsibilities 2000 miles apart, the issue came down to *realistic choices vs. romantic ones.* Eventually, Bunny said, "Why can't we just romance reality?"

We're still looking for a way to romance that reality. We don't want to belittle the real challenges, but we don't want to ignore the reality of our romance either -- and that reality is gaining weight against the other ones every day.

Like Alice, we can't deny what is — no matter how strange it becomes. Yet, that conviction itself can lead to some pretty bizarre places. One strange reality that lovers might face occasionally is how to deal with anger. You love this person, and still you're angry at them. What do you do? You romance that reality.

While "strange" may always be a constant in Wonderland, sometimes we can shift it from "upsetting strange" to "fun and exciting strange." That whole territory of how good friends deal with bad feelings is one of those areas that can get "curiouser and curiouser" the further you go into it.

It's hard for me to imagine ever getting mad at my sweet little Bunny. Usually, when I start going off in a nonconstructive direction, she'll just say, "Hunny, hunny, hunny…" until I stop talking. It feels like I'm being kissed until I shut up. She brings me back to a happier and more relevant reality, and it's over.

However, she asked once about how we should handle that awkward situation when one of us gets mad for one reason or another. I had to admit that I'd given some thought to the idea of how intimate friends might handle that problem in an intimate way—thoughts that were undoubtedly the result of having too much time alone to fantasize.

Bunny and I had already agreed that we'd prefer not be reasonable in matters of love whenever there's a more romantic or even a more creative option available. Also, as far as I'm concerned, talking should be used for trying to express our love for each other. Once there's anger, I figure it's because someone feels taken advantage of in some inappropriate way. So, theoretically, maybe the best way to take care of those feelings of being violated is to agree that the offended person can take physical control of the offending party.

Talking when you're in that space can lead to some seriously hurt feelings. So, why not just sublimate all that anger into something that might lead back to love?

I told Bunny that if she ever gets mad at me, just slap me, throw me down, and take me. I may struggle a little, but not so much that she can't do what she has to do to feel better.

She said she probably wouldn't do that because she knows I'd like it. (I don't think she could actually do that anyway, but it is fun to think about.) After talking about that a bit, I think we agreed that the purpose of the exercise isn't to punish the other person, but to resolve the anger, so we can talk constructively and lovingly again. So this way of dealing with things does make sense (at least to me). It's one of those ways we can step outside of our normal patterns of making sense out of a situation and jump-start our sense of a better sense.

I think it's an important first step to realize that we never want to punish our partner, no matter how we decide to handle the difficult situations. We just want to work out our issues, so we can get back to our Wonderland—where our delight with each other grows with every step.

Realize that we are all essentially loving beings, and are simply visitors to this land of confusing realities and nonsense that controls the lives of so many others. Also, we don't come here empty handed. We bring with us the magic of love and the creative power of Wonderland—and our own innate sense of "sense."

Romance is optimistic and creative. Those who dwell in the world of inescapable cold, hard realities tend to be reactive. How else can you behave when you believe that the most important factors in the entire real world are all outside of yourself?

A person with a romantic mindset will look at their external reality and think outside the lines a bit. They'll say, "Yeah, but..." Or sometimes, we may not like what we see at all, and think, as Alice did that, "That was the silliest tea party I ever went to! I am never going back there again!"

However, while we're still at the party, might as well have fun with it. We do what we can in a creative way. And when we allow hope and other romantic notions to elevate us above our reactive minds, miracles happen and a happier *sense* begins!

George Bernard Shaw once said that "Life isn't about finding yourself. It's about creating yourself." And creating yourself is sometimes about turning nonsense into sense, or as Bunny put it, about "romancing reality."

Revelation 10: If we don't romance reality, we end up as whatever helpless heap the chaotic external "reality" molds us into all by itself.

No one wants to be a helpless heap. Still, we've all been there to some degree before we take the leap of faith off the merry-go-round.

I was pretty discouraged by my life prospects a while back, and I didn't really feel like trying much anymore. Nothing seemed worth the effort. In a desperate moment, I sent out a prayer, and it felt like I connected to God, or my higher self, or someone, who then responded. I said I needed help, and that I would renew my efforts to do my best during this strange tea party if he/they could send me someone to make life easier and happier. I thought that was reasonable, and I felt that he/they did too.

In fact, by the time I was done, it seemed to me that we had struck a deal.

Months later (in June of 2012), I wrote this to remind myself of that deal: *I will not... {and} I will work faithfully to bring about the goals of the hierarchy, and I will be given a woman to ground me, stabilize me, and give me peace and joy. It's in the works and I need to anti-up by working faithfully until that relationship can manifest. She will be a deep well of love and reassurance, and all will be well. But it won't happen unless I keep moving forward faithfully.*

So, with that reminder to myself, I did my best to keep up my end of the deal, and on October 23 (four months after writing that note to myself) I met Bunny. Of course, I quickly fell madly in love with her, but more than that, I felt strangely relieved—instantly, as soon as we started talking.

I wrote in chapter three that after reviewing the files of many online romantic prospects, I summed up each one of them in a one-line statement: "I have kids, but it could work;" "I just wanna play;" "I need someone, anyone;" "I don't need anyone, but go ahead and try to talk to me..."

What I heard when I looked at Bunny's picture was, "I'll take care of you. No problem." That stopped me in my tracks.

After finding my note from last June, it now seems like maybe God or someone was speaking through her to let me know that the Universe will take care of me and that she's a big part of that. Sure, I'll keep doing my part, but that's super easy now. Everything is easy when you know you're loved.

That's a romantic notion, but I firmly believe it's one that can totally give our cold, cruel world the sense it needs. Love can take the heaviest realities and make them light. Love is literally the difference between Heaven and Hell. And although many say that we should be able to feel love for life all by ourselves, having a cooperative partner definitely multiplies that ability.

Some say that you can't depend on anyone but yourself. In fact, I think that current generally accepted wisdom states that we have everything inside ourselves that we need, and we simply need to get used to stop feeling sorry for ourselves and not look to anyone else for any help. While that may be a spiritually valid notion in the sense that there are no excuses for not taking responsibility for our own lives, I think that it's also an idea that's desperately in need of romancing.

Love should be an attainable goal. Personally, I think it's a necessary one if we hope to scale more than halfway up the pyramid of needs. Also, since like attracts like (sooner or later), I think that acting like the kind of person we want to attract must eventually result in the perfect partner—perfect for learning what we need to learn, anyway. Then, when we're a better person, we'll attract a better partner, or help create one out of what we've got.

Walking in this world confronts us with constant challenges. The reality of our own deficiencies, and the shortcomings of others, is inescapable. A loving partner who can help us find enough bliss and strength to happily jump back into the world of difficult choices again is a real blessing. It's a miracle, that gives us the strength and perspective to create our own miracles.

It's always difficult when life seems to be a choice between acting in either a realistic way or a romantic one. I know which one I prefer. Still, sometimes romantic notions just aren't realistic, which I'd still be fine with, as long as they still make some sort of sense. However, perhaps you can imagine the problem when the chosen path dead ends into totally unworkable situations—at least until we do a little work on them.

Buddha was the first to suggest that we walk the middle path. This is where we find bliss through detachment (occasionally). Other times, it's a very uncomfortable place as we do our best to refrain from identifying with either side. In this dualistic world, there are always two sides, and the dynamics of that complexity is what gives depth to our experience here.

When I start getting too blissful, Bunny will playfully remind me of the challenges we face by saying something like, "You're white and I'm black."

I always hate that because that makes it sound like we're totally different—as different as black and white. We're actually so much alike that I tend to think of us as twins. When I look at her, it's like looking at a mirror. She's exactly like me, just a little darker. Then Bunny snaps me back to the realization of our differences.

I never knew how to handle that until I woke up to the realization that she's also a girl and I'm a guy. That's pretty different, too. Still, if that's okay, then our skin-deep difference sure should be okay. That's one way I romance reality in my own mind in order to shape it into something I can live with. It may sound like a rationalization, but to me it's a life-altering joyful perspective that makes me okay with the persistence of reality.

Therefore, romantic rationalizations are realistic. They're ultra-realistic, because they have the power to bring real life into an otherwise sad existence. It's all part of the wondrous, transformational logic of love.

The Logic of Love

"I'm afraid I can't explain myself, sir. Because I am
not myself, you see?"
~Lewis Carroll, Alice in Wonderland

"I'm a little pencil in the hands of God who is
scripting his love letter to the world."
~Mother Teresa

We each script God's love letter to the world in
our own way—as soon as we let the hand of
God help us get the lead out.

Alice made her mark in Wonderland by being
flexible enough to work with the new rules she found
in there. Flexibility also provides love with room to
maneuver, so its logic can unfold and work its magic
on our lives.

A loving companion can not only help us achieve
goals that we may not be able to reach on our own,
but their love can also transport us to a much better

place. It can clear the clouds from the sky and fill our lives with sunshine. It can open the gate to a garden blooming with beauty that illuminates the soul. There's profound and compelling logic to a relationship that fills us with the peace, strength and wonder that only love can create.

Bunny and I often discussed the realities that keep us from the reducing the two thousand miles between us. She has a good supervisory job that she'd have to quit if she moved here, and I have a daughter who will be a senior in high school next year, so I can't move there. That's the reality. Still, "the heart wants what the heart wants" and I feel that I have no choice but to listen.

Reality may take a little romancing, and personally, I'm hoping for a miracle—another miracle, I guess. Still, we have to follow the logic that love dictates, so we can stay happily productive, and have the energy that love creates to keep climbing up to the pinnacle of the pyramid where we can be of most use to ourselves and others.

At the heart of the logic of love is

Revelation #6: Restated, it's the idea that Love empowers us to be our best.

It sustains us and motivates us to keep on trying when giving up would be much more reasonable. At the peak of the pyramid, love transforms us from a mere mortal to a self-actuating force to be reckoned with – a force of nature, integrated into the whole but with distinctly individualized characteristics.

Love can turn a regular schmo into a saint. Well, even if some people come into this world a little higher up the evolutionary ladder than others, love is what keeps their boat afloat. No matter who you are, love is what makes conviction possible—even when people that we have to deal with are unreasonable, self-centered and irritating in every possible way.

"People are often unreasonable and self-centered. Forgive them anyway.
If you are kind, people may accuse you of ulterior motives. Be kind anyway.
If you are honest, people may cheat you. Be honest anyway.
If you find happiness, people may be jealous. Be happy anyway.
The good you do today may be forgotten tomorrow. Do good anyway.
Give the world the best you have and it may not be good enough. Give your best anyway."
~Mother Teresa

Do you think Mother T would be nearly this saintly if she weren't supported and motivated by love? Also, the love she demonstrated worked absolute miracles—in a hands-on way—and in the sense that she inspired so many more people to be their best.

So it's logical to be kind even when people accuse you of ulterior motives; be honest even when people cheat you; be happy even when it brings out jealousy in others; and do good even when it's not always good enough, and in spite of the fact that people will probably quickly forget a lot of the good you do. Why? Because

Revelation 11: Love is an absolute miracle maker, for yourself and the world.

It takes real conviction to consistently do the right thing. Love gives us the strength and desire to do that. So fortified with love, our promises to ourselves can then become the mortar that holds our foundational convictions in place.

Personal Promises, My Anchor to Wonderland

"It was much pleasanter at home," thought poor Alice, "when one wasn't always growing larger and smaller, and being ordered about by mice and rabbits. I almost wish I hadn't gone down the rabbit-hole—and yet—and yet..."

~Lewis Carroll, Alice in Wonderland

. . . And yet, once love opens our eyes to Wonderland, no other world is ever good enough again. Love has raised me up, making me huge, ignorantly aloof and blissful, and love lost in the past has reduced me to a smaller person than I ever thought possible.

Still, just as becoming very small helped Alice get places she could never have gone otherwise, being reduced by loss builds humility and helps us rebuild our lives on much more solid foundations. No one likes being ordered around by mice and rabbits—or selfish, gluttonous pigs, for that matter. Yet, as Mother Teresa put it, "be kind anyway."

Love supports us in our convictions, and following through on our convictions in turn feeds that love. So, our convictions and promises actually anchor us in this very special world.

Bunny and I made some promises to each other the second day after we met, before we'd actually even talked on the phone. When I asked her what she was looking for in a relationship, she said she just wanted someone who would kiss her every day.

See how I got hooked? I replied that if we ever got together, I could promise her three things:

1. I promise to give you regular hugs and kisses every day.

2. I'll do my best to always feed our heart in open and honest ways, so we continue to delight in getting closer all the time. And,

3. I promise to start and end each day with hugs and kisses, so our love always grows deeper.

Well, then there was no turning back. Although we were separated by half of the country and a lot of other realities that would totally deter any sane person, we kept talking and making more promises to each other.

Although we're both very romantic, we also both slipped into occasionally talking about our possibilities together from a reasonable standpoint. That always brought me down, so I made Bunny another promise.

"I will always speak to your heart in the language it understands, and to avoid reason and reality at all costs."

Avoiding reason and reality is quite a goal. I think I'm up it, but while I was still pondering the wisdom of that conviction, Bunny sent me a note that felt like a particularly poetic promise. She says she's going to include it in her wedding vows to me. It's a quote from Pablo Neruda:

"I love you without knowing how, or when, or from where. I love you simply, without problems or pride: I love you in this way because I do not know any other way of loving but this, in which there is no I or you, so intimate that your hand upon my chest is my hand, so intimate that when I fall asleep your eyes close."

That's so true. Her hand seems like my hand often, and when she falls asleep, I can finally close my eyes.

When I wake up, I know I'm going to be the man that wakes up next to her. And if I grow old, if I EVER grow old, I know I'm going to be the man that grows old with her. I'd walk 1000 miles, and I'd walk 1000 more just to be the man who walked 2000 miles (from Montana to Memphis) to fall down at her door. (My attempt at poetry, paraphrased from the old classic, "500 miles")

That's basically how we ended up in Wonderland. At first, I was really surprised by how open she was with me. I was even more surprised when I heard from her family and friends about how her walls kept most guys out (over the last 30 years since her divorce). I didn't feel any walls at all, and I was amazed how brave she was to be so very open. She thought I was really brave, too, by coming to Memphis on Thanksgiving and meeting her at the same time I met her family.

At any rate, we soon found ourselves welded together at the heart, and nothing besides love has seemed very important by comparison ever since.

Of course this love extends to our kids, family, and friends. It fills us and extends out to the whole world—the whole universe, which now seems to have been magically transformed into a Wonderland.

It extends to mice and rabbits, (both white and black), strange and objectionable characters of all kinds. Love has made the world a gentler and more beautiful place, and best of all, it's self-perpetuating.

Revelation 12: When we feel love, we extend kindness, which generates more love. It's God's perpetual motion machine.

> *"Kindness in words creates confidence.*
> *Kindness in thinking creates profundity.*
> *Kindness in action creates love."*
> *~Lao Tzu*

Everything in Wonderland is all about love! I carries its own logic, expresses itself in its own language, and I personally know that it has the power to breathe vitality into even the dullest life.

Revelation 7 (restated): Love is the magic cookie that makes even the smallest person a giant.

Tea Time

"I wish I hadn't cried so much!" said Alice, as she swam about, trying to find her way out. I shall be punished for it now, I suppose, by being drowned in my own tears !"

~Lewis Carroll, Alice in Wonderland

There there... Everything is going to be fine. You won't drown if you stop crying. And you can join in the fun anytime.

Revelation 13: "It's always tea time" (ever since the Mad Hatter had an argument with Time.) And everyone is welcome—as long as you mind your manners and play nice.

Below are translations of the *play nice* rule. There may be many cultures, but there's still only one Golden Rule:

Baha'i Faith

Lay not on any soul a load that you would not wish to be laid upon you, and desire not from anyone the things you would not desire for yourself ~ *Baha'u'llan, Gleanings*

Christianity

All things whatsoever ye would that men should do to you, do ye so to them. *Matthew 7:1*

Confucianism

Do not do to others what you would not like yourself. Then there will be no resentment against you, either in the family or in the state. *Analects 12:2*

Buddhism

Hurt not others in ways that you yourself would find hurtful. *Adana-Vargas 5,1*

Hinduism

This is the sum of duty; do naught onto others what you would not have them do unto you. *Mahabharata 5,1517*

Islam

No one of you is a believer until he desires for his brother that which he desires for himself. *Sun nah*

Jainism

One should treat all creatures in the world as one would like to b e treated. ~ *Mahavira, Sutrakritanga*

Judaism

What is hateful to you, do not do to your fellowman. This is the entire Law; all the rest is commentary. *Talmud, Sabbath 3id*

Sikhism

I am a stranger to no one; and no onel is a stranger to me. Indeed, I am a friend to all. ~ *Gutu Granth Sahib, Pg 1299*

Taoism

Regard your neighbor's gain as your gain, and your neighbor's loss as your own loss. *Tai Shang Kan Yin P'ien*

Zoroastrianism (600 BCE)

That nature alone is good which refrains from doing another whatsoever is not good for itself. Dadisten-I-dinik, 94,5 and "Whatever is disagreeable to yourself, do not do unto others. *Shast-na-shayast 13:29*

And finally, speaking for the religion of Science, Linus Pauling, peace activist and two-time Nobel prize winner: *"Do unto others 20% better than you would expect them to do unto you, to correct for subjective error."*

"It's always tea time." We just have to stop crying, drop whatever silly notions that keep us from getting along with others, and try a little harder to play nice.

"Once more she found herself in the long hall, and close to the little glass table. 'Now, I'll manage better this time,' she said to herself, and began by taking the little golden key, and unlocking the door that led into the garden. ... she walked down the little passage, and THEN, she found herself at last in the beautiful garden, among the bright flower-beds and the cool fountains." -from Alice In Wonderland

"When you make loving others the story of your life, there's never a final chapter, because the legacy continues. You lend your light to one person, and he or she shines it on another and another and another."

– Oprah Winfrey

The Golden Key

"My dear, here we must run as fast as we can,
just to stay in place.
And if you wish to go anywhere, you must run
twice as fast as that."

~Lewis Carroll, Alice in Wonderland

Running as fast as I can and not getting anywhere is the story of my life. How are we supposed to "run twice as fast as that?"

Running faster than we can in order to get anywhere sounds absurd, and yet it rings true somehow. So what's the key?

Sure, landing in Wonderland can be as simple and easy as falling down a bunny hole. Still, once you find yourself there, the rules can be baffling.

For instance, when the fairer sex says "we need to talk," what she probably means is that she needs to complain. Or when she says, "Do what you want,"

more than likely, that means "You'll pay for it later."
When she says "NO," of course it means "No," but it
can also mean "Yes" or "Maybe." But "Maybe" almost
always means "No."

This strange land has a strange language all it's
own. It may seem like nonsense, but when you look
closely, you see that it works (when it works) on the
logic of love.

How do you run twice as fast as you can? It's
impossible, right?

Not if there are two of you. That's the key that
many insist is unnecessary. Still, in your heart, you
know that love is absolutely the most necessary thing
in the world.

So top off your tanks with that supercharging
additive, because the race against that other reality is
about to begin.

One key to an amazing and lasting relationship
is to regularly remind yourself what you like about
your partner. Short lists are great because they're easy
to remember. But longer lists are good for those days
when the short one just isn't good enough.

For instance, if your only reason for being with
someone is "because he makes me laugh," someday,
you'll think, "*He's just not funny anymore; I'm outta here.*"

Remembering one or two things daily that you
like best about your partner is a great idea. However,
you might want to keep a secret list at the bottom of
your underwear drawer that you occasionally refer to
and update as realizations occur to you.

For instance, I remind myself regularly of a couple simple things that I love best about Bunny.

1. She let's me kiss her and hold her as
much as I want.

2. She understands me, accepts me, and
somehow still seems to love me deeply.

However, I also have a list extension that took a little more thought, and I plan to keep putting thought into it for the rest of my life.

This is sort of a personal list, but I'm sharing my secret thoughts with you, so you get the idea how to make your own list. Then, as you and your partner compare lists, happy agreements will result that then become the basis of your promises to each other.

Here's my underwear drawer list to date:

3. She says "Whatever you want, Hunny,"
often, and her devotion to my happiness is
very convincing.

4. I can be completely honest with her,
saying things any way that occurs to me
without getting in trouble. She encourages
this and she actually reminds me often that
she loves our talks.

5. I can even share my deep-seated fears, foibles, and fantasies that are next to impossible to understand even for me!

6. She's not fooled by my image of myself. Even when I'm feeling ugly or awkward, she seems pleased with me. She makes me feel whole when I feel broken and simply innocent when I thought I was dumb.

7. Although we both believe in not staying in a relationship that is not happy and harmonious, she's promises to never leave me—and when I get worried, she doesn't seem to mind renewing that promise.

8. She lets me lose myself in a dream as we cuddle, happily hugging and caressing mostly unconsciously.
I guess that's enough for you to get the idea.

Here's Bunny's list:

I love him because.....

1. He wants to touch and kiss my chocolate skin all the time.

2. He grabs me for hugs and kisses whenever I'm near him.

3. He likes it when I work my womanly wiles on him and trusts me enough to know that I won't take advantage of that fact.

4. He needs me.

5. He has a funny dry sense of humor that I love, and he doesn't think he's funny.

6. He will discuss the fact that I am black and he is white, and what that may mean, even though that's a subject that he doesn't like to talk about.

7. He has a wonderful mind, and he challenges me to use my mind in different ways than I would have otherwise.

8. He's the only man I know that would even let me think about building my dream house with the green door and thatch roof.

It really helped me to see this. I think these lists reveal priorities about the other that neither of us suspected.

Sometimes, it's hard to believe we're worthy of the loving partner we want and need. I know I'm old, and Bunny keeps pointing out that, on top of that, I'm white. I also know myself to be a pretty quirky animal.

I growl when I'm pleased, and wag my tail when I'm angry. Therefore I'm mad.'

'I call it purring, not growling,' said Alice." —Ah, the voice of love....

Another voice of love once told Bunny (in answer to her prayers), "*Take care of him. He needs you.*"

At first, she thought it was God talking to her. Then, the image of the guide became increasingly clear to her in future conversations. Love has opened her mind to new possibilities, and she told me it stretches her heart every day so it's big enough to accomodate her growning love.

Those are the times when it's hard to feel worthy. I was basically looking for comfort when I first fell into the Bunny hole. I landed in a strange world where the rules and rewards were much different than anything I'd ever known.

That eventually led to Revelation 14: the logic of love often necessitates the avoidance of reason...

Because logic deprived of the influence of love can severely handicap our optimism and creativity. I've learned how love and lightness can be self-perpetuating to the point that it creates an entirely new, and much more beautiful, world.

We just need to keep feeding the love with faith. That can be a challenging prospect when you think about it. Having faith in uncertain prospects is a little scary, and doubt is bound to be a constant companion. Still, I think it's the key, and for me it's as simple as knowing that I'd follow the magnificant soul in my little black Bunny anywhere.

Having someone who makes the complications in life simple and the difficult lessons easy is an absolute

Godsend. For that matter, "God" is another of those conplicated concepts, but love is simple, and it's all we really need to know, or believe in, to make the blessings of "God" work. We can debate about what we don't know, but when we talk about what we do know from the heart, we find the common ground that IS Wonderland.

Then, we recognize that we have help being more than we thought we were. Cooperation may just be the little brother of love, but it transforms each of us and our world into a much gentler and more beautiful place. Suddenly, we can run twice as fast as we otherwise could, and we can and finally get somewhere.

When you live with the realization of this kind of care and conern, life isn't a competition anymore. You realize that what looks like a race to others is simply an exercise to test and build your creativity and endurance.

Revelation 15: Relationships are actually divinely mystical and cooperative efforts where every troublesome person around you becomes your partner.

Your endurance and creativity is multiplied when you're supported by an emotionally intimate accountable partner. Many don't believe this is necessary or even possible—like many don't believe in God anymore. However, belief isn't what's necessary.

In a word, the golden key that unlocks the gates to this satisfying, successful, wonderous land is love. And in two words, the key to not getting locked out of this lovingly cooperative Wonderland is, "*Yes, dear.*"

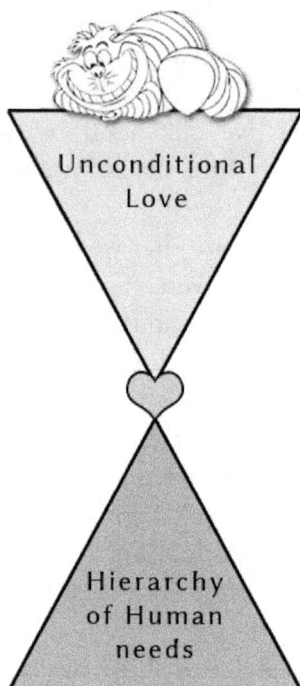

Those two words speak volumes about the value of having a co-captain to help me navigate the rest of my journey – a journey that's begun with a complete transformation. As Bunny and I walk hand in hand into Wonderland, the great narrator in my head whispers a warning that this is not merely the beginning of a new chapter in my life. Life as I knew it is now over, and my co-editor is helping me write an entirely new story.

We were each beginning our twilight years when we met. Yet, we somehow brought out the vulnerability and trust of newborns in each other. Soon, we moved on to a childlike hope and optimism, and then onto the excitement of teenagers in love. Still a helpless kid, I'm powerless to do anything but totally surrender.

I tried to describe what my reincarnation into this land of sunshine and moonbeams had done for me in sensible terms. Yet, this key that unlocked my heart didn't just help me scale the hierarchy of human needs. It's opened the door to a world of divine cooperation that defies description—an invisible, inverted pyramid (crazy, upside-down world) that begins where human needs end.

The 15 Revelations

In the human world, you have 10 Commandments. In this crazy Wonderland world, we have 15 Revelations – and they all have to do with LOVE.

1. Black is not as different as it might seem from white.

2. Accepting the differences between ourselves and others broadens our horizons and deepens our soul.

3. The most important relationship technique is to sincerely care about the other person more than your own ego

4. Learning to care about something bigger than yourself is what growing up is all about.

5. Love has a life all its own that is more important than any individual life involved.

6. The goal of carefully and faithfully applying the transformational power of love results in nothing

short of life liberating, soul satisfying salvation!

7. A good relationship gives you confidence in your abilities and helps you stay inspired to do and be your best.

> Easy to remember version: Love empowers us to be our best.

> "Love is the magic cookie that makes even the smallest person a giant!"

8. When the feminine force is allowed to fill the minds of men, our worlds don't crash when they collide anymore. They bounce with joy, and everyone celebrates the miraculous reunion.

9. Despite how religiously many hang onto their beliefs, the deepest beliefs are still only skin-deep compared to the love for all that's rooted in our infinite source.

10. If we don't romance reality, we end up as whatever helpless heap the chaotic external "reality" molds us into all by itself.

11. Love is an absolute miracle maker, for yourself and the world.

12. When we feel love, we extend kindness, which generates more love. It's God's perpetual motion machine.

13. "It's always tea time." We just have to stop crying, drop whatever silly notions that keep us from getting along, and try a little harder to play nice.

14. The logic of love often necessitates the avoidance of reason

15. Relationships are actually divinely mystical and cooperative efforts where every troublesome person around you becomes your partner.

Out-takes

The working title of this book was *Hunt 'n Bunny in Wonderland,* and this was what we figured we'd use for the cover:

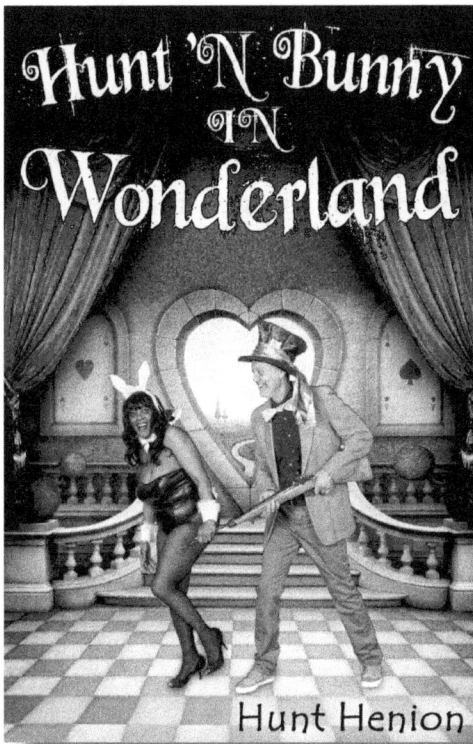

Friends loved it, but when I sent the manuscript to professionals, I got comments back using words like, "sexist, "too provocative," "politically incorrect...."

I was also told I absolutely can't have a gun on the front cover. No gun would make my title, *Hunt 'n Bunny,* meaningless. I had thought of *hunting bunny* as a sort of metaphor for looking for love. Also, since my love was named Bunny (making us *Hunt & Bunny)*, I thought the title was perfect.

After being corrected by a few pros, I conceded that I must be wrong, but just for the record, Bunny never did. We were having fun – too much fun evidently to think clearly about public perceptions. Still, I just thought I'd take our discarded title and cover out of the trash for those who like to know about the bloopers.

We were also strongly advised to never show any of the following pictures, because they all have the "confusing imagery" of a rifle in them:

We took about 50 pictures like this, and we can't use any of them, because they carry "sexist connotations" magnified by having me (the male chauvinist) in the "dominant position."

So... we threw away the *Hunt 'n Bunny* concept because I don't want to create any barriers to anyone's understanding of the *relationship revelations* that I present in these pages.

Still, my own biggest revelation is that however the censors edit my work and life, I know now that I'll always stumble along somehow, happily Hunt 'n Bunny.

Other Books by
Hunt Henion

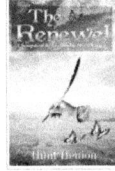

Looking, Seeing & Knowing
(Barns and Noble Best seller)

The Don Q Point Of View

The BIG Fake-out, The Illusion of Limits

Books Compiled by Hunt Henion

The Sacred Shift, Co-Creating Your Future in a New Renaissance and
2012, Creating Your Own Shift
(Both #1 Amazon Bestsellers)

www.shiftawareness.com

www.ingramcontent.com/pod-product-compliance
Lightning Source LLC
LaVergne TN
LVHW021520080426
835509LV00018B/2581